MW01537318

If found, pls. return this planner to:

____

____

____

"Behind every happy child is a loving babysitter".

2019

January

Sun	Mon	Tue	Wed	Thu	Fri	Sat
30	31	1	2	3	4	5
6	7	8	9	10	11	12
13	14	15	16	17	18	19
20	21	22	23	24	25	26
27	28	29	30	31	1	2
3	4	5	6	7	8	9

February

Sun	Mon	Tue	Wed	Thu	Fri	Sat
27	28	29	30	31	1	2
3	4	5	6	7	8	9
10	11	12	13	14	15	16
17	18	19	20	21	22	23
24	25	26	27	28	1	2
3	4	5	6	7	8	9

March

Sun	Mon	Tue	Wed	Thu	Fri	Sat
24	25	26	27	28	1	2
3	4	5	6	7	8	9
10	11	12	13	14	15	16
17	18	19	20	21	22	23
24	25	26	27	28	29	30
31	1	2	3	4	5	6

April

Sun	Mon	Tue	Wed	Thu	Fri	Sat
31	1	2	3	4	5	6
7	8	9	10	11	12	13
14	15	16	17	18	19	20
21	22	23	24	25	26	27
28	29	30	1	2	3	4
5	6	7	8	9	10	11

May

Sun	Mon	Tue	Wed	Thu	Fri	Sat
28	29	30	1	2	3	4
5	6	7	8	9	10	11
12	13	14	15	16	17	18
19	20	21	22	23	24	25
26	27	28	29	30	31	1
2	3	4	5	6	7	8

June

Sun	Mon	Tue	Wed	Thu	Fri	Sat
26	27	28	29	30	31	1
2	3	4	5	6	7	8
9	10	11	12	13	14	15
16	17	18	19	20	21	22
23	24	25	26	27	28	29
30	1	2	3	4	5	6

July

Sun	Mon	Tue	Wed	Thu	Fri	Sat
30	1	2	3	4	5	6
7	8	9	10	11	12	13
14	15	16	17	18	19	20
21	22	23	24	25	26	27
28	29	30	31	1	2	3
4	5	6	7	8	9	10

August

Sun	Mon	Tue	Wed	Thu	Fri	Sat
28	29	30	31	1	2	3
4	5	6	7	8	9	10
11	12	13	14	15	16	17
18	19	20	21	22	23	24
25	26	27	28	29	30	31
1	2	3	4	5	6	7

September

Sun	Mon	Tue	Wed	Thu	Fri	Sat
1	2	3	4	5	6	7
8	9	10	11	12	13	14
15	16	17	18	19	20	21
22	23	24	25	26	27	28
29	30	1	2	3	4	5
6	7	8	9	10	11	12

October

Sun	Mon	Tue	Wed	Thu	Fri	Sat
29	30	1	2	3	4	5
6	7	8	9	10	11	12
13	14	15	16	17	18	19
20	21	22	23	24	25	26
27	28	29	30	31	1	2
3	4	5	6	7	8	9

November

Sun	Mon	Tue	Wed	Thu	Fri	Sat
27	28	29	30	31	1	2
3	4	5	6	7	8	9
10	11	12	13	14	15	16
17	18	19	20	21	22	23
24	25	26	27	28	29	30
1	2	3	4	5	6	7

December

Sun	Mon	Tue	Wed	Thu	Fri	Sat
1	2	3	4	5	6	7
8	9	10	11	12	13	14
15	16	17	18	19	20	21
22	23	24	25	26	27	28
29	30	31	1	2	3	4
5	6	7	8	9	10	11

2020

January

Sun	Mon	Tue	Wed	Thu	Fri	Sat
29	30	31	1	2	3	4
5	6	7	8	9	10	11
12	13	14	15	16	17	18
19	20	21	22	23	24	25
26	27	28	29	30	31	1
2	3	4	5	6	7	8

February

Sun	Mon	Tue	Wed	Thu	Fri	Sat
26	27	28	29	30	31	1
2	3	4	5	6	7	8
9	10	11	12	13	14	15
16	17	18	19	20	21	22
23	24	25	26	27	28	29
1	2	3	4	5	6	7

March

Sun	Mon	Tue	Wed	Thu	Fri	Sat
1	2	3	4	5	6	7
8	9	10	11	12	13	14
15	16	17	18	19	20	21
22	23	24	25	26	27	28
29	30	31	1	2	3	4
5	6	7	8	9	10	11

April

Sun	Mon	Tue	Wed	Thu	Fri	Sat
29	30	31	1	2	3	4
5	6	7	8	9	10	11
12	13	14	15	16	17	18
19	20	21	22	23	24	25
26	27	28	29	30	1	2
3	4	5	6	7	8	9

May

Sun	Mon	Tue	Wed	Thu	Fri	Sat
26	27	28	29	30	1	2
3	4	5	6	7	8	9
10	11	12	13	14	15	16
17	18	19	20	21	22	23
24	25	26	27	28	29	30
31	1	2	3	4	5	6

June

Sun	Mon	Tue	Wed	Thu	Fri	Sat
31	1	2	3	4	5	6
7	8	9	10	11	12	13
14	15	16	17	18	19	20
21	22	23	24	25	26	27
28	29	30	1	2	3	4
5	6	7	8	9	10	11

July

Sun	Mon	Tue	Wed	Thu	Fri	Sat
28	29	30	1	2	3	4
5	6	7	8	9	10	11
12	13	14	15	16	17	18
19	20	21	22	23	24	25
26	27	28	29	30	31	1
2	3	4	5	6	7	8

August

Sun	Mon	Tue	Wed	Thu	Fri	Sat
26	27	28	29	30	31	1
2	3	4	5	6	7	8
9	10	11	12	13	14	15
16	17	18	19	20	21	22
23	24	25	26	27	28	29
30	31	1	2	3	4	5

September

Sun	Mon	Tue	Wed	Thu	Fri	Sat
30	31	1	2	3	4	5
6	7	8	9	10	11	12
13	14	15	16	17	18	19
20	21	22	23	24	25	26
27	28	29	30	1	2	3
4	5	6	7	8	9	10

October

Sun	Mon	Tue	Wed	Thu	Fri	Sat
27	28	29	30	1	2	3
4	5	6	7	8	9	10
11	12	13	14	15	16	17
18	19	20	21	22	23	24
25	26	27	28	29	30	31
1	2	3	4	5	6	7

November

Sun	Mon	Tue	Wed	Thu	Fri	Sat
1	2	3	4	5	6	7
8	9	10	11	12	13	14
15	16	17	18	19	20	21
22	23	24	25	26	27	28
29	30	1	2	3	4	5
6	7	8	9	10	11	12

December

Sun	Mon	Tue	Wed	Thu	Fri	Sat
29	30	1	2	3	4	5
6	7	8	9	10	11	12
13	14	15	16	17	18	19
20	21	22	23	24	25	26
27	28	29	30	31	1	2
3	4	5	6	7	8	9

Child's Name

Date

6 am	
7	
8	
9	
10	
11	
12 pm	
1	
2	
3	
4	
5	
6	
7	
8	

Priorities

Notes

Parent's Contact Info.

Child's Name

Date

6 am	
7	
8	
9	
10	
11	
12 pm	
1	
2	
3	
4	
5	
6	
7	
8	

Priorities

Notes

Parent's Contact Info.

Child's Name

Date

6 am	
7	
8	
9	
10	
11	
12 pm	
1	
2	
3	
4	
5	
6	
7	
8	

Priorities

Notes

Parent's Contact Info.

Child's Name

Date

6 am	
7	
8	
9	
10	
11	
12 pm	
1	
2	
3	
4	
5	
6	
7	
8	

Priorities

Notes

Parent's Contact Info.

Child's Name

Date

6 am	
7	
8	
9	
10	
11	
12 pm	
1	
2	
3	
4	
5	
6	
7	
8	

Priorities

Notes

Parent's Contact Info.

Child's Name

Date

6 am	
7	
8	
9	
10	
11	
12 pm	
1	
2	
3	
4	
5	
6	
7	
8	

Priorities

Notes

Parent's Contact Info.

Child's Name

Date

6 am	
7	
8	
9	
10	
11	
12 pm	
1	
2	
3	
4	
5	
6	
7	
8	

Priorities

Notes

Parent's Contact Info.

Child's Name

Date

6 am	
7	
8	
9	
10	
11	
12 pm	
1	
2	
3	
4	
5	
6	
7	
8	

Priorities

Notes

Parent's Contact Info.

Child's Name

Date

6 am	
7	
8	
9	
10	
11	
12 pm	
1	
2	
3	
4	
5	
6	
7	
8	

Priorities

Notes

Parent's Contact Info.

Child's Name

Date

6 am	
7	
8	
9	
10	
11	
12 pm	
1	
2	
3	
4	
5	
6	
7	
8	

Priorities

Notes

Parent's Contact Info.

Child's Name

Date

6 am	
7	
8	
9	
10	
11	
12 pm	
1	
2	
3	
4	
5	
6	
7	
8	

Priorities

Notes

Parent's Contact Info.

Child's Name

Date

6 am	
7	
8	
9	
10	
11	
12 pm	
1	
2	
3	
4	
5	
6	
7	
8	

Priorities

Notes

Parent's Contact Info.

Child's Name

Date

6 am	
7	
8	
9	
10	
11	
12 pm	
1	
2	
3	
4	
5	
6	
7	
8	

Priorities

Notes

Parent's Contact Info.

Child's Name

Date

6 am	
7	
8	
9	
10	
11	
12 pm	
1	
2	
3	
4	
5	
6	
7	
8	

Priorities

Notes

Parent's Contact Info.

Child's Name

Date

6 am	
7	
8	
9	
10	
11	
12 pm	
1	
2	
3	
4	
5	
6	
7	
8	

Priorities

Notes

Parent's Contact Info.

Child's Name

Date

6 am	
7	
8	
9	
10	
11	
12 pm	
1	
2	
3	
4	
5	
6	
7	
8	

Priorities

Notes

Parent's Contact Info.

Child's Name

Date

6 am	
7	
8	
9	
10	
11	
12 pm	
1	
2	
3	
4	
5	
6	
7	
8	

Priorities

Notes

Parent's Contact Info.

Child's Name

Date

6 am	
7	
8	
9	
10	
11	
12 pm	
1	
2	
3	
4	
5	
6	
7	
8	

Priorities

Notes

Parent's Contact Info.

Child's Name

Date

6 am	
7	
8	
9	
10	
11	
12 pm	
1	
2	
3	
4	
5	
6	
7	
8	

Priorities

Notes

Parent's Contact Info.

Child's Name

Date

6 am	
7	
8	
9	
10	
11	
12 pm	
1	
2	
3	
4	
5	
6	
7	
8	

Priorities

Notes

Parent's Contact Info.

Child's Name

Date

6 am	
7	
8	
9	
10	
11	
12 pm	
1	
2	
3	
4	
5	
6	
7	
8	

Priorities

Notes

Parent's Contact Info.

Child's Name

Date

6 am	
7	
8	
9	
10	
11	
12 pm	
1	
2	
3	
4	
5	
6	
7	
8	

Priorities

Notes

Parent's Contact Info.

Child's Name

Date

6 am	
7	
8	
9	
10	
11	
12 pm	
1	
2	
3	
4	
5	
6	
7	
8	

Priorities

Notes

Parent's Contact Info.

Child's Name

Date

6 am	
7	
8	
9	
10	
11	
12 pm	
1	
2	
3	
4	
5	
6	
7	
8	

Priorities

Notes

Parent's Contact Info.

Child's Name

Date

6 am	
7	
8	
9	
10	
11	
12 pm	
1	
2	
3	
4	
5	
6	
7	
8	

Priorities

Notes

Parent's Contact Info.

Child's Name

Date

6 am	
7	
8	
9	
10	
11	
12 pm	
1	
2	
3	
4	
5	
6	
7	
8	

Priorities

Notes

Parent's Contact Info.

Child's Name

Date

6 am	
7	
8	
9	
10	
11	
12 pm	
1	
2	
3	
4	
5	
6	
7	
8	

Priorities

Notes

Parent's Contact Info.

Child's Name

Date

6 am	
7	
8	
9	
10	
11	
12 pm	
1	
2	
3	
4	
5	
6	
7	
8	

Priorities

Notes

Parent's Contact Info.

Child's Name

Date

6 am	
7	
8	
9	
10	
11	
12 pm	
1	
2	
3	
4	
5	
6	
7	
8	

Priorities

Notes

Parent's Contact Info.

Child's Name

Date

6 am	
7	
8	
9	
10	
11	
12 pm	
1	
2	
3	
4	
5	
6	
7	
8	

Priorities

Notes

Parent's Contact Info.

Child's Name

Date

6 am	
7	
8	
9	
10	
11	
12 pm	
1	
2	
3	
4	
5	
6	
7	
8	

Priorities

Notes

Parent's Contact Info.

Child's Name

Date

6 am	
7	
8	
9	
10	
11	
12 pm	
1	
2	
3	
4	
5	
6	
7	
8	

Priorities

Notes

Parent's Contact Info.

Child's Name

Date

6 am	
7	
8	
9	
10	
11	
12 pm	
1	
2	
3	
4	
5	
6	
7	
8	

Priorities

Notes

Parent's Contact Info.

Child's Name

Date

6 am	
7	
8	
9	
10	
11	
12 pm	
1	
2	
3	
4	
5	
6	
7	
8	

Priorities

Notes

Parent's Contact Info.

Child's Name

Date

6 am	
7	
8	
9	
10	
11	
12 pm	
1	
2	
3	
4	
5	
6	
7	
8	

Priorities

Notes

Parent's Contact Info.

Child's Name

Date

6 am	
7	
8	
9	
10	
11	
12 pm	
1	
2	
3	
4	
5	
6	
7	
8	

Priorities

Notes

Parent's Contact Info.

Child's Name

Date

6 am	
7	
8	
9	
10	
11	
12 pm	
1	
2	
3	
4	
5	
6	
7	
8	

Priorities

Notes

Parent's Contact Info.

Child's Name	Date

6 am	
7	
8	
9	
10	
11	
12 pm	
1	
2	
3	
4	
5	
6	
7	
8	

Priorities

Notes

Parent's Contact Info.

Child's Name

Date

6 am	
7	
8	
9	
10	
11	
12 pm	
1	
2	
3	
4	
5	
6	
7	
8	

Priorities

Notes

Parent's Contact Info.

Child's Name

Date

6 am	
7	
8	
9	
10	
11	
12 pm	
1	
2	
3	
4	
5	
6	
7	
8	

Priorities

Notes

Parent's Contact Info.

Child's Name

Date

6 am	
7	
8	
9	
10	
11	
12 pm	
1	
2	
3	
4	
5	
6	
7	
8	

Priorities

Notes

Parent's Contact Info.

Child's Name

Date

6 am	
7	
8	
9	
10	
11	
12 pm	
1	
2	
3	
4	
5	
6	
7	
8	

Priorities

Notes

Parent's Contact Info.

Child's Name

Date

6 am	
7	
8	
9	
10	
11	
12 pm	
1	
2	
3	
4	
5	
6	
7	
8	

Priorities

Notes

Parent's Contact Info.

Child's Name

Date

6 am	
7	
8	
9	
10	
11	
12 pm	
1	
2	
3	
4	
5	
6	
7	
8	

Priorities

Notes

Parent's Contact Info.

Child's Name

Date

6 am	
7	
8	
9	
10	
11	
12 pm	
1	
2	
3	
4	
5	
6	
7	
8	

Priorities

Notes

Parent's Contact Info.

Child's Name

Date

6 am	
7	
8	
9	
10	
11	
12 pm	
1	
2	
3	
4	
5	
6	
7	
8	

Priorities

Notes

Parent's Contact Info.

Child's Name

Date

6 am	
7	
8	
9	
10	
11	
12 pm	
1	
2	
3	
4	
5	
6	
7	
8	

Priorities

Notes

Parent's Contact Info.

Child's Name

Date

6 am	
7	
8	
9	
10	
11	
12 pm	
1	
2	
3	
4	
5	
6	
7	
8	

Priorities

Notes

Parent's Contact Info.

Child's Name

Date

6 am	
7	
8	
9	
10	
11	
12 pm	
1	
2	
3	
4	
5	
6	
7	
8	

Priorities

Notes

Parent's Contact Info.

Child's Name

Date

6 am	
7	
8	
9	
10	
11	
12 pm	
1	
2	
3	
4	
5	
6	
7	
8	

Priorities

Notes

Parent's Contact Info.

Child's Name

Date

6 am	
7	
8	
9	
10	
11	
12 pm	
1	
2	
3	
4	
5	
6	
7	
8	

Priorities

Notes

Parent's Contact Info.

Child's Name

Date

6 am	
7	
8	
9	
10	
11	
12 pm	
1	
2	
3	
4	
5	
6	
7	
8	

Priorities

Notes

Parent's Contact Info.

Child's Name

Date

6 am	
7	
8	
9	
10	
11	
12 pm	
1	
2	
3	
4	
5	
6	
7	
8	

Priorities

Notes

Parent's Contact Info.

Child's Name

Date

6 am	
7	
8	
9	
10	
11	
12 pm	
1	
2	
3	
4	
5	
6	
7	
8	

Priorities

Notes

Parent's Contact Info.

Child's Name

Date

6 am	
7	
8	
9	
10	
11	
12 pm	
1	
2	
3	
4	
5	
6	
7	
8	

Priorities

Notes

Parent's Contact Info.

Child's Name

Date

6 am	
7	
8	
9	
10	
11	
12 pm	
1	
2	
3	
4	
5	
6	
7	
8	

Priorities

Notes

Parent's Contact Info.

Child's Name

Date

6 am	
7	
8	
9	
10	
11	
12 pm	
1	
2	
3	
4	
5	
6	
7	
8	

Priorities

Notes

Parent's Contact Info.

Child's Name

Date

6 am	
7	
8	
9	
10	
11	
12 pm	
1	
2	
3	
4	
5	
6	
7	
8	

Priorities

Notes

Parent's Contact Info.

Child's Name

Date

6 am	
7	
8	
9	
10	
11	
12 pm	
1	
2	
3	
4	
5	
6	
7	
8	

Priorities

Notes

Parent's Contact Info.

Child's Name

Date

6 am	
7	
8	
9	
10	
11	
12 pm	
1	
2	
3	
4	
5	
6	
7	
8	

Priorities

Notes

Parent's Contact Info.

Child's Name

Date

6 am	
7	
8	
9	
10	
11	
12 pm	
1	
2	
3	
4	
5	
6	
7	
8	

Priorities

Notes

Parent's Contact Info.

Child's Name

Date

6 am	
7	
8	
9	
10	
11	
12 pm	
1	
2	
3	
4	
5	
6	
7	
8	

Priorities

Notes

Parent's Contact Info.

Child's Name

Date

6 am	
7	
8	
9	
10	
11	
12 pm	
1	
2	
3	
4	
5	
6	
7	
8	

Priorities

Notes

Parent's Contact Info.

Child's Name

Date

6 am	
7	
8	
9	
10	
11	
12 pm	
1	
2	
3	
4	
5	
6	
7	
8	

Parent's Contact Info.

Priorities

Notes

Child's Name

Date

6 am	
7	
8	
9	
10	
11	
12 pm	
1	
2	
3	
4	
5	
6	
7	
8	

Priorities

Notes

Parent's Contact Info.

Child's Name

Date

6 am	
7	
8	
9	
10	
11	
12 pm	
1	
2	
3	
4	
5	
6	
7	
8	

Priorities

Notes

Parent's Contact Info.

Child's Name

Date

6 am	
7	
8	
9	
10	
11	
12 pm	
1	
2	
3	
4	
5	
6	
7	
8	

Priorities

Notes

Parent's Contact Info.

Child's Name

Date

6 am	
7	
8	
9	
10	
11	
12 pm	
1	
2	
3	
4	
5	
6	
7	
8	

Priorities

Notes

Parent's Contact Info.

Child's Name

Date

6 am	
7	
8	
9	
10	
11	
12 pm	
1	
2	
3	
4	
5	
6	
7	
8	

Priorities

Notes

Parent's Contact Info.

Child's Name

Date

6 am	
7	
8	
9	
10	
11	
12 pm	
1	
2	
3	
4	
5	
6	
7	
8	

Priorities

Notes

Parent's Contact Info.

Child's Name

Date

6 am	
7	
8	
9	
10	
11	
12 pm	
1	
2	
3	
4	
5	
6	
7	
8	

Priorities

Notes

Parent's Contact Info.

Child's Name

Date

6 am	
7	
8	
9	
10	
11	
12 pm	
1	
2	
3	
4	
5	
6	
7	
8	

Priorities

Notes

Parent's Contact Info.

Child's Name

Date

6 am	
7	
8	
9	
10	
11	
12 pm	
1	
2	
3	
4	
5	
6	
7	
8	

Priorities

Notes

Parent's Contact Info.

Child's Name

Date

6 am	
7	
8	
9	
10	
11	
12 pm	
1	
2	
3	
4	
5	
6	
7	
8	

Priorities

Notes

Parent's Contact Info.

Child's Name

Date

6 am	
7	
8	
9	
10	
11	
12 pm	
1	
2	
3	
4	
5	
6	
7	
8	

Priorities

Notes

Parent's Contact Info.

Child's Name

Date

6 am	
7	
8	
9	
10	
11	
12 pm	
1	
2	
3	
4	
5	
6	
7	
8	

Priorities

Notes

Parent's Contact Info.

Child's Name

Date

6 am	
7	
8	
9	
10	
11	
12 pm	
1	
2	
3	
4	
5	
6	
7	
8	

Priorities

Notes

Parent's Contact Info.

Child's Name

Date

6 am	
7	
8	
9	
10	
11	
12 pm	
1	
2	
3	
4	
5	
6	
7	
8	

Priorities

Notes

Parent's Contact Info.

Child's Name

Date

6 am	
7	
8	
9	
10	
11	
12 pm	
1	
2	
3	
4	
5	
6	
7	
8	

Priorities

Notes

Parent's Contact Info.

Child's Name

Date

6 am	
7	
8	
9	
10	
11	
12 pm	
1	
2	
3	
4	
5	
6	
7	
8	

Priorities

Notes

Parent's Contact Info.

Child's Name

Date

6 am	
7	
8	
9	
10	
11	
12 pm	
1	
2	
3	
4	
5	
6	
7	
8	

Priorities

Notes

Parent's Contact Info.

Child's Name

Date

6 am	
7	
8	
9	
10	
11	
12 pm	
1	
2	
3	
4	
5	
6	
7	
8	

Priorities

Notes

Parent's Contact Info.

Child's Name

Date

6 am	
7	
8	
9	
10	
11	
12 pm	
1	
2	
3	
4	
5	
6	
7	
8	

Priorities

Notes

Parent's Contact Info.

Child's Name

Date

6 am	
7	
8	
9	
10	
11	
12 pm	
1	
2	
3	
4	
5	
6	
7	
8	

Priorities

Notes

Parent's Contact Info.

Child's Name

Date

6 am	
7	
8	
9	
10	
11	
12 pm	
1	
2	
3	
4	
5	
6	
7	
8	

Priorities

Notes

Parent's Contact Info.

Child's Name

Date

6 am	
7	
8	
9	
10	
11	
12 pm	
1	
2	
3	
4	
5	
6	
7	
8	

Priorities

Notes

Parent's Contact Info.

Child's Name

Date

6 am	
7	
8	
9	
10	
11	
12 pm	
1	
2	
3	
4	
5	
6	
7	
8	

Priorities

Notes

Parent's Contact Info.

Child's Name

Date

6 am	
7	
8	
9	
10	
11	
12 pm	
1	
2	
3	
4	
5	
6	
7	
8	

Priorities

Notes

Parent's Contact Info.

Child's Name

Date

6 am	
7	
8	
9	
10	
11	
12 pm	
1	
2	
3	
4	
5	
6	
7	
8	

Priorities

Notes

Parent's Contact Info.

Child's Name

Date

6 am	
7	
8	
9	
10	
11	
12 pm	
1	
2	
3	
4	
5	
6	
7	
8	

Priorities

Notes

Parent's Contact Info.

Child's Name

Date

6 am	
7	
8	
9	
10	
11	
12 pm	
1	
2	
3	
4	
5	
6	
7	
8	

Priorities

Notes

Parent's Contact Info.

Contacts

Name ____________ Address ____________ ____________ City ________ State ________ Zip ________ Phone # ________ Email ____________	Name ____________ Address ____________ ____________ City ________ State ________ Zip ________ Phone # ________ Email ____________
Name ____________ Address ____________ ____________ City ________ State ________ Zip ________ Phone # ________ Email ____________	Name ____________ Address ____________ ____________ City ________ State ________ Zip ________ Phone # ________ Email ____________
Name ____________ Address ____________ ____________ City ________ State ________ Zip ________ Phone # ________ Email ____________	Name ____________ Address ____________ ____________ City ________ State ________ Zip ________ Phone # ________ Email ____________
Name ____________ Address ____________ ____________ City ________ State ________ Zip ________ Phone # ________ Email ____________	Name ____________ Address ____________ ____________ City ________ State ________ Zip ________ Phone # ________ Email ____________
Name ____________ Address ____________ ____________ City ________ State ________ Zip ________ Phone # ________ Email ____________	Name ____________ Address ____________ ____________ City ________ State ________ Zip ________ Phone # ________ Email ____________

Contacts

Name ______ Address ______ ______ City ______ State ______ Zip ______ Phone # ______ Email ______	Name ______ Address ______ ______ City ______ State ______ Zip ______ Phone # ______ Email ______
Name ______ Address ______ ______ City ______ State ______ Zip ______ Phone # ______ Email ______	Name ______ Address ______ ______ City ______ State ______ Zip ______ Phone # ______ Email ______
Name ______ Address ______ ______ City ______ State ______ Zip ______ Phone # ______ Email ______	Name ______ Address ______ ______ City ______ State ______ Zip ______ Phone # ______ Email ______
Name ______ Address ______ ______ City ______ State ______ Zip ______ Phone # ______ Email ______	Name ______ Address ______ ______ City ______ State ______ Zip ______ Phone # ______ Email ______
Name ______ Address ______ ______ City ______ State ______ Zip ______ Phone # ______ Email ______	Name ______ Address ______ ______ City ______ State ______ Zip ______ Phone # ______ Email ______

Contacts

Name ____

Address ____

____

City __________________ State____________

Zip __________ Phone # __________________

Email ___________________________________

Name ____

Address ____

____

City __________________ State____________

Zip __________ Phone # __________________

Email ___________________________________

Name ____

Address ____

____

City __________________ State____________

Zip __________ Phone # __________________

Email ___________________________________

Name ____

Address ____

____

City __________________ State____________

Zip __________ Phone # __________________

Email ___________________________________

Name ____

Address ____

____

City __________________ State____________

Zip __________ Phone # __________________

Email ___________________________________

Name ____

Address ____

____

City __________________ State____________

Zip __________ Phone # __________________

Email ___________________________________

Name ____

Address ____

____

City __________________ State____________

Zip __________ Phone # __________________

Email ___________________________________

Name ____

Address ____

____

City __________________ State____________

Zip __________ Phone # __________________

Email ___________________________________

Name ____

Address ____

____

City __________________ State____________

Zip __________ Phone # __________________

Email ___________________________________

Name ____

Address ____

____

City __________________ State____________

Zip __________ Phone # __________________

Email ___________________________________

Made in the USA
Las Vegas, NV
06 January 2022

40621875R00057